Learn Spanish For Beginners

Learn Spanish Effortlessly With Simple Lessons To Practice

Marcus Rodriguez

4

TABLE OF CONTENTS

INTRODUCTION 7

UN TIEMPO PARA VOLAR **18**

    PREGUNTAS (QUESTIONS) 23

    RESPUESTAS (ANSWERS) 24

SOFIA Y LA SOPA MAGICA **26**

    PREGUNTAS (QUESTIONS) 29

    RESPUESTAS (ANSWERS) 29

LOS MURCIÉLAGOS DEL SEÑOR DOMSON **31**

    VOCABULARIO 31

    PREGUNTAS (QUESTIONS) 41

    RESPUESTAS (ANSWERS) 42

¿TE CONOZCO? - DO I KNOW YOU? **44**

    VOCABULARY 44

    RESPUESTAS (ANSWERS) 47

EL PUEBLO DE CALAVERA **49**

    VOCABULARIO 56

    PREGUNTAS DE SELECCIÓN MÚLTIPLE 56

    RESPUESTAS AL CAPÍTULO 1 57

INTRODUCTION

ESPAÑA

Conjugating Verbs

CONJUGATING =
MAKING A VERB AGREE
WITH ITS SUBJECT

3 *kinds of verbs:*

	-AR	-ER	-IR
start with infinitive:	HABLAR (TO SPEAK)	COMER (TO EAT)	VIVIR (TO LIVE)
remove ending:	HABL -AR STEM ENDING	COM -ER STEM ENDING	VIV -IR STEM ENDING
add ending to stem:	HABL +	COM +	VIV +

SUBJECT PRONOUNS

YO	NOSOTROS
TÚ	VOSOTROS
ÉL, ELLA, UD.	ELLOS(AS), UDS.

-AR ENDINGS	
-O	-AMOS
-AS	-ÁIS
-A	-AN

-ER ENDINGS	
-O	-EMOS
-ES	-ÉIS
-E	-EN

-IR ENDINGS	
-O	-IMOS
-ES	-ÍS
-E	-EN

✳ Spanish411.net

YO HABLO (I SPEAK)	TÚ COMES (YOU EAT)	ELLOS VIVEN (THEY LIVE)

Spanish Irregular Verbs

Present Tense Reference Chart / Quiz or Worksheet

By Sue Summers

Spanish
AR Verbs

2 Game Boards
and Vocabulary

By Sue Summers

Over the last several centuries, Spanish has been across multiple continents and forged connections between all of them. Spanish has persisted as a linguistic force since the Spanish empire began to cover the world over. The language spoken now isn't quite the same as the language spoken in the 15th century on the first voyage to the new world, but the similarities between that variety of Spanish and the modern-day variety of Spanish sets you up for libraries worth of literature from all over the world in the Spanish language.

Due to many long stretches of communication with the British and as a result of normal antiquated progenitors, Spamish has offered English-speakers a genuinely simple way to bantering utilizing an alternate language. Spanish and English offer a few likenesses in sentence development. You may even understand that a great deal of Spanish and English words has comparable sounds. The restricted French sounds may in any case be natural to you in light of films and TV shows.

A portion of these one of a kind Spanish sounds incorporate the quiet "h" and the rough "r" sound; however, this doesn't totally imply that all that you watch and hear on TV is absolutely precise. In any case, having the option to receive the Spanish articulation you have procured from watching films can help you a great deal while learning the language.

Just like the English spoken in the United States, the English spoken in Australia, and the English spoken in England are vastly different, likewise is the Spanish of Spain, the Spanish of Mexico, and the Spanish of, say, Argentina. They're different in manner of accent and dialect and some basic things, such as the usage of "vosotros" in Castilian Spanish

(Castellano), or the Spanish of mainland Spain, where instead "ustedes" is used in Latin American Spanish. There's also the fact that certain dialects use the pronoun vos, which is generally never used otherwise and sounds rather booky and antiquated in the same way that using the pronoun thou sound in English.

These dialects were made from the Latin language utilized by the Romans during their attacks in 1 B.C.; yet notwithstanding their normal root, the development of the Spanish language is not quite the same as the advancement of Italian and French (which despite everything share a great deal of similitudes even up to today).

This book contains demonstrated advances and methodologies on the best way to begin learning the Spanish language. I trust that through this book, you will pick up the certainty to begin learning another dialect, regardless of how old you are. Try not to stress on the off chance that you have not yet taken in any unknown dialect previously. In this book, you will locate the fundamental standards of the language which can make it simpler for you to assemble expressions and sentences in French. You will learn fundamental expressions, yet additionally French letters in order, sentence development, just as articulation. There are numerous explanations behind needing to become familiar with the Spanish language rapidly. You should locate the correct inspiration and wonder why you're keen on learning Spanish. Possibly you will travel soon, or you want to serve your locale better. It may be the case that you need to upgrade your resume or, just, to extend your points of view by getting a subsequent language. Whatever your reasons, learning Spanish can be a satisfying undertaking.

Interfacing with others and our condition is the way we took in our local dialects as infants. Likewise, tuning in and associating with people around us help structure our jargon and information. The explanation that connection works when learning another dialect is that it is basic, and it's common.

There is a hypothesis in language that when learning another dialect as an intuitive procedure between a student and a local speaker, correspondence and familiarity are handily accomplished. It is on the grounds that the local speaker adjusts the language and makes it simpler for you as an apprentice to become familiar with the language. The capable speaker will utilize known jargon, talking gradually and obviously. The local speaker will modify the point, stay away from sayings, and utilize less complex linguistic structures. Thusly, the information encourages you with a superior comprehension of the Spanish language.

With more than 400 million local Spanish speakers around the world, Spanish is the official language of 21 nations and is the second most-communicated in language on the planet! Remember that you should try sincerely and focus on concentrated investigation meetings to have the option to convey in Spanish rapidly. We start by setting a practical cutoff time and making a learning plan. When you have an arrangement set up, you should begin acquainting yourself with fundamental jargon words that you can later expand upon. Next, finding an online program, guide, class, or application that will give you access to both sound and visual learning. Having a decent blend of instructional materials will assist with keeping you responsible and on target. One of the most basic parts of rapidly learning another dialect is to inundate yourself in the language as much as possible. At long last, practice increasingly visit so you can speak in light of other Spanish speakers — keeping that the objective is to comprehend the Spanish language rather than simply deciphering it.

In this book, we will concentrate on furnishing you with words written in Spanish and English. These words will be utilized in a sentence in Spanish, which we will likewise convert into English with the goal that you can investigate the setting in the two dialects. Through this, you will have the option to look at the importance of every one of the words, concentrating on only each in turn.

For example:

Hola / Hello

Hola, ¿Cómo estas? / Hello, how are you?

Here, the main word is hola, which is the word initially mentioned, while the rest of the words are what we call context. Thanks to this method, you will learn to use the main word in context and also the meaning of the secondary words.

In the following lessons, you will find words from different topics, such as verbs, adjectives, adverbs, polysemous words, home, household chores, clothes, garments, accessories, nature, animals, professions, family, relationships, numbers, and many more. Learning these words and knowing how to use them will upgrade your Spanish language to the intermediate level.

Spanish has a very different system of pronunciation to English. It's far more regular but also a fair bit more nuanced in the specific sounds. With the espoused regularity of Spanish pronunciation comes a fair amount of adjustment from our English alphabet where a given letter can stand in for any number of different sounds.

We recommend reviewing the words provided here in the book at least once every two months so that you can remember them and put them into practice in your everyday life.

There are plenty of books on this subject on the market, so thank you again for choosing this one! Every effort was made to ensure it is full of as much useful information as possible. Please enjoy!

UN TIEMPO PARA VOLAR

Había una tendencia opresiva en el pueblo de Hilton Valley, donde todas las cabezas se inclinaban ante Kala, una mafia callejera. Timi no disfrutó su tercer encuentro con Kala esa semana, pero aun así, luchó contra ello, sin dejar ir su dinero bien ganado.

"Siéntate sin moverte", la voz de Jane hizo eco en la cabeza adolorida de Tim mientras ella limpiaba su ceja con un paño húmedo.

"Esta es la tercera vez que peleas esta semana", dijo Jane.

"¿Qué le hiciste a Kala esta vez?", preguntó.

Escurrió agua del paño y lo colocó nuevamente en su cabeza.

"Nada" respondió Timi.

Murmuró por lo bajo.

Jane dejó el paño en un bowl con agua que tenia en sus piernas, mientras atendía la cabeza de Timi.

"¿Qué hacemos ahora?" murmuró también.

"Si te pudieron hacer esto a ti, seguramente van a venir por mi." Su voz era solo un suspiro, pero sonaba como truenos en la cabeza de Timi.

Timi recogió el vaso de agua que estaba al pie de la cama en la habitación pobremente iluminada, y tomó dos tabletas de analgésicos.

Jane debe haberlas comprado en el mostrador.

"Tenemos que enfrentarnos a estos matones", hablo Timi con rabia.

"¿Por qué tengo que pagar para vivir? ¿qué clase de vida es esa? No es diferente a la esclavitud", puso su cabeza entre sus manos y gimió.

Su cuerpo parecía incapaz de sostener su discurso apasionado.

Jane lo besó en la frente y empujó sus hombros a la cama.

"¡Descansa, hermano! Te ves horrible ahora", dijo.

Timi tenía un ojo morado, y los labios rotos.

Había dejado de sangrar gracias a Jane, pero le dolía como cuando 10 hormigas molestas deciden alimentarse con tu carne.

Su ojo izquierdo estaba hinchado, y necesitaba una bolsa de hielo.

Pero el hielo era una comodidad escasa.

Apenas habían logrado pagar el gas el mes pasado.

La vida no se suponía que fuese tan difícil, pero un nombre hacía que todos temblaran de miedo en Hilton Valley, "Kala".

"Te dejaré dormir ahora. Deberías sentirte un poco mejor en la mañana", dijo Jane.

Besó su frente y dejó la habitación

Timi sonrió mientras se fue.

Su hermana menor era un ángel, y Timi la había protegido de toda opresión.

Con apenas 22 años, Timi era responsable de Jane de 19 años.

Deseaba poderle dar mas, pero estaban endeudados.

Todos en Hilton Valley estaban endeudados, excepto Kala.

Tenían que pagar le 20% de sus ingresos diarios como impuesto de seguridad.

Tim trato de voltear los ojos al pensar en su deuda, pero se estremeció del dolor.

Era paradójico.

Tenían que pagarle a Kala impuesto de seguridad por protección, para que no les golpeara o destruyera su hogar.

Timi no podía pagar eso.

Necesitaba todo el dinero porque mantener a Jane, su salud y bienestar dependían de ello.

No le importaba salir golpeado para proteger a su hermana menor..

Ok, ahora hagamos un ejercicio rápido: te haré 5 preguntas. Trata de responder y luego de las preguntas, te daré las respuestas.

A Time to Fight

There was an oppressive trend in the town of Hilton Valley, where all heads bowed to Kala, an influential street Mafia.

Timi didn't enjoy his third-time encounter with Kala this week, but still, he fought it out, without letting go of his hard-earned money.

"Sit still," Jane's voice echoed in Timi's pain-filled head as she mopped his brow with a damp cloth.

"This is the third time you've been in a fight this week," said Jane.

"What did you do to Kala this time?" She asked further.

She wrung water out of the cloth and placed it back on his head.

"Nothing," Timi replied.

He mumbled under his breath.

Jane dropped the cloth in the bowl of water, she had placed on her lap, as she tended Timi's head.

"What do we do now?" She mumbled too.

"If they could do this to you, they will surely come for me." Her voice was just a whisper, but it sounded like the crack of thunder in Timi's head.

Timi picked up the glass of water sitting on the footstool in his dimly lit bedroom and swallowed two painkiller tablets.

Jane must have bought them over the counter.

"We have to stand up to these bullies," Timi spoke in anger.

"Why do I have to pay to live? What kind of life is that? This is no different from slavery." He held his head with his hands and moaned.

His body seemed incapable of handling his passionate speech.

Jane kissed him on his head and pushed his shoulders down onto the bed.

"Rest, brother! You look horrible right now," she said.

Timi had a black eye, and his lips were split.

It had stopped bleeding thanks to Jane, but it hurt like when ten angry ants decide to feast on your flesh.

His left eye was swollen, and he needed an ice pack.

But ice was a scarce commodity.

They had barely managed to pay for gas the previous month.

Life wasn't supposed to be this hard, but one name made everyone in Hilton Valley tremble with fear, 'Kala'.

"I will let you sleep now. You should feel a little better in the morning," said Jane.

She kissed his forehead and left the room.

Timi smiled as she left.

His little sister was such an angel, and Timi had to protect her from all oppression by any means.

Barely 22, Timi was responsible for 19-year-old Jane.

He wished he could provide more, but they were in debt.

Everyone in Hilton Valley was in debt except Kala.

You had to pay him 20% of your daily earnings as a security levy.

Timi tried to roll his eyes over his debt, but he winced from the pain.

It was so paradoxical.

You had to pay Kala security levy as protection, so he wouldn't beat you up or destroy your livelihood.

Timi couldn't afford that.

He needed all the money because Jane's upkeep, health, and welfare depended on it.

He didn't mind getting beaten up to shield his baby sister.

Ok let's now start a quick exercise: I am going to ask you 5 questions. Try to reply and after the questions, I will give you the answers.

Preguntas (Questions)
1.¿Por qué Jane estaba atendiendo la cabeza de Timi?

2.¿Cuántas veces Timi había estado en una pelea esa semana?

3.¿Quién es Jane para Timi?

4.¿Por qué Timi se negaba a renunciar a sus ganancias?

5.¿Por la historia, puedes ver que Kala era un _____?

1. Why was Keysha tending Timi's head?

2. How many times had Timi been in a fight that week?

3. Who is Keysha to Timi?

4. Why did Timi refuse to give up his earnings?

5. From the story, you can see that Kala was a _____?

Respuestas (Answers)

1. Porque tuvo una herida en una pelea con Kala

2. 3 veces

3. Su hermana

4. Necesitaba el dinero para mantener a Jane, su salud y bienestar.

5. Un matón

1. He received an injury from a fight with Kala

2. Three times

3. His sister

4. He needed the money for Jane's upkeep, health, and welfare.

5. Bully

SOFIA Y LA SOPA MAGICA

S ofia es una niña que está en segundo año en una escuela llamada "Vivaldi Escuela Internacional".

Sofia tiene 15 y está muy triste porque todas sus amigas de la escuela tienen novios. Ella no.

Un buen día decidió que era tiempo de cambiar y ser hermosa.

"Abuela, ¿cómo puedo ser hermosa?" le preguntó a su abuela.

"Sofia, tú eres hermosa, pero si quieres ser aún más hermosa tienes que comer una sopa mágica. Es una sopa especial que sirve para ser hermosa.

Sofia inmediatamente comenzó a buscar recetas y finalmente encontró la receta que estaba buscando en una revista. Se llamaba "la sopa de la belleza" y era fácil de cocinar.

Una tarde cuando llegó de la escuela, empezó a hacer su sopa mágica. Tomó el sartén y puso papas, zanahorias, sal, pimienta y mucho más. Tenía muy buen olor y el fuego estaba alto. 5 minutos antes de terminar, sonó el timbre. Sofia fue a abrir la puerta, y ahí estaba John, el chico más guapo de la escuela. Sofia había estado enamorada de John por un largo tiempo y lo había invitado a su casa esa tarde, pero nunca hubiese pensado que John realmente la visitaría.

"Hola Sofia. Huele muy bien", dijo John.

Sofia respondió, "Gracias John. Estará listo pronto y podremos probarlo"

Los minutos restantes pasaron rápido, y Sofia y John hablaron mucho. John parecía muy interesado en Sofia.

"Ok, la sopa está lista", dijo Sofia y comenzó a servirla en los platos.

Cuando John la probó, le dijo: "Sofia, esta es la mejor sopa que he probado". Se levantó y empezó a besar a Sofia. El sueño de Sofia se hizo realidad, como si por magia se hubiese vuelto la novia del chico más guapo de la escuela.

Ok, ahora hagamos un ejercicio rápido: te haré 3 preguntas. Trata de responder y luego de las preguntas, te daré las respuestas.

Sofia and the Magic Soup

Sofia is a girl who attends the second-grade class, in a school called "Vivaldi International School".

Sofia was 15 and very sad because her school's friends all had boyfriends. She didn't.

One fine day she decided it was time to change and become beautiful.

"Grandma, how can I become beautiful?" She asked her grandmother.

"Sofia you are beautiful but if you want to become even more beautiful you will have to eat a magic soup. It is a special soup that helps you to become beautiful "

Sofia immediately started looking for recipes and finally found the recipe she was looking for in a magazine. It was called "The soup of beauty" and was easy to cook.

One afternoon when she came home from school, she immediately started cooking her magic soup. She took the pan and put in potatoes, carrots, salt, pepper and much more. The smell was very good and the heat was turmed up high. It was 5 minutes before it would be ready, when the doorbell rang. Sofia went to open the door and there was John, the most beautiful boy in the school. Sofia had been in love with John for a long time and had invited him to her house that afternoon but she had never thought that John would really visit her.

"Hi Sofia, what a nice smell," said John

Sofia replied, "Thanks John, it will be ready soon and we can taste it."

The remaining minutes passed quickly and Sofia and John talked a lot. John seemed very interested in Sofia.

"Ok the soup is ready," said Sofia and started pouring it into the dishes.

As soon as John tasted it, he said: "Sofia this is the best soup I've ever tasted". He stood up and started kissing Sofia. Sofia's dream came true, and as if by magic she became the girlfriend of the most beautiful boy in the school.

Ok let's now start a quick exercise: I am going to ask you 3 questions. Try to reply and after the questions, I will give you the answers.

Preguntas (Questions)

1. ¿Cuántos años tenía Sofia?

2. ¿Cuál era el nombre del chico más guapo de la escuela?

3. ¿Cuál era el nombre de la receta de sopa?

1. How old was Sofia?

2. What is the name of the most beautiful boy in the school?

3. What was the name of the soup recipe?

Respuestas (Answers)

1. 15

2. John

3. La sopa de la belleza

1. 15

2. John

3. The soup of beauty

LOS MURCIÉLAGOS
DEL SEÑOR DOMSON

Vocabulario

aberrante (ah-beh-rrahn-teh) Adjective - unusual

aclararles (ah-klah-rahr-lehs) Transitive verb - to clarify

agudizar (ah-goo-dee-sahr) Transitive verb - to sharpen

ahuyentaba (ow-yehn-tah-bah) Transitive verb - frightened off

ala (ah-lah) Feminine noun - wing

arrancaba (ah-rrahn-kah-bah) Transitive verb - to pull out

bandada (bahn-dah-dah) Feminine noun - flock

camioneta (kah-myoh-neh-tah) Feminine noun - van

centeno (sehn-teh-noh) Masculine noun - rye

ciego (syeh-goh) Adjective - blind

confundiéndose (kohm-foon-dee-ehn-doh-sey) Transitive verb - to be confused

criar (kryahr) Transitive verb - to raise

cuatrocientos ochenta (kwah-troh-syehn-tohs oh-chehn-tah) Adjective - four-hundred eighty

despidieron (dehs-peh-dee-rohn) Transitive verb - they said goodbye

31

dotado (doh-tah-doh) Adjective - gifted

fenómeno (feh-noh-meh-noh) Masculine noun - a phenomenon

granja (grahng-hah) Feminine noun - farm

gruesa (grweh-sah) Feminine noun - twelve dozen

guacamaya (gwah-kah-mah-yah) Feminine noun - macaw

hallaron (ah-yah-rohn) Transitive verb - they found

huerto (wehr-toh) Masculine noun - a vegetable garden

infelices (eem-feh-lee-sehs) Adjective - unhappy

jardín (hahr-deen) Masculine noun - garden

mamífero (mah-mee-feh-roh) Masculine noun - mammal

manicomio (mah-nee-koh-myoh) Masculine noun - asylum

mediocridad (meh-dyoh-kree-dahd) Feminine noun - mediocrity

metido (meh-tee-doh) Adjective - involved

pariente (pah-ryehn-teh) Masculine or Feminine noun - relative, family member

periodista (peh-ryoh-dees-tah) Masculine or Feminine noun - journalist

picada (pee-kah-dah) Feminine noun - snack

piedra (pyeh-drah) Feminine noun - stone

prensa (prehn-sah) Feminine noun - press

psiquiátrico (see-kyah-tree-koh) Adjective - psychiatric

quirópteros (kee-rohp-teh-rohs) Plural noun - bats

relacionarse (rreh-lah-syoh-nahr-seh) Pronominal verb - to have contact

ruego (rrweh-goh) Masculine noun - a plea

sano (sah-noh) Adjective - healthy

suceso (soo-seh-soh) Masculine noun - event

tapados (tah-pah-dohs) Transitive verb - to cover

trozo (troh-soh) Masculine noun - piece

vergonzoso (behr-gohn-soh-soh) Adjective - shameful

Todas las noches a las 11 en punto Domson que tenía ocho años salía al patio de su casa y al **jardín**. Se quedaba quieto en silencio, observando el árbol que estaba al frente porque sabía que ahí estaba siempre colgado de cabeza un murciélago. Le gustaba verlo volar y perderse, **confundiéndose** con la oscuridad de la noche. Todos los murciélagos se parecen y además vuelan juntos en grandes **bandadas**, pero Domson estaba seguro de que siempre veía al mismo murciélago. Tenía la misma capacidad que tienen estos **mamíferos**, un sistema de ultrasonido de alta frecuencia. Domson era un niño especial **dotado** de grandes facultades y una de ellas era que se podía guiar y localizar cualquier dirección por medio de los sonidos. Todas las noches a las 11 Domson le ponía unos **trozos** de fruta **picada** al murciélago. El tiempo pasó y el pequeño niño de ocho años creció. Ahora Domson era un señor de 40 años y nunca dejó de **relacionarse** con los murciélagos. Desarrolló un vínculo fuerte con los murciélagos, una conexión especial. El entendía a los murciélagos y los murciélagos lo entendían a él. Era una comunicación perfecta, mucho mejor y más sincera que la que tienen los humanos. Toda la vida Domson fue víctima de burlas y humillaciones por amar tanto a los murciélagos. Creían que estaba **metido** en algún culto satánico pero Domson nunca le prestó atención a esos ataques porque sabía que eran producto de la ignorancia y la **mediocridad**.

Domson trabajaba en una agencia de publicidad y mercadeo pero lo dejó todo para dedicarse al estudio de estos **quirópteros**. Agarró todos sus ahorros y compró una granja para **criar**, cuidar y recibir a los murciélagos que llegaban de todas partes. Era un hombre solitario: no se había casado ni tenía pareja o tenía amigos. Su única compañía eran los murciélagos. Tan íntima y fuerte era la relación que tenía con ellos que con el tiempo desarrolló las mismas costumbres - dormía colgado de cabeza y se alimentaba solo de frutas y pan de **centeno**.

No era **ciego**. Tenía una buena vista y sus ojos estaban muy **sanos**. Sin embargo, pasaba días enteros con los ojos **tapados** con una tela negra **gruesa** para desarrollar y **agudizar** sus otros sentidos. Cada vez se parecía más a un murciélago y menos a un humano. Pero lo verdaderamente extraño era que a veces los murciélagos parecían humanos. Aprendieron a pronunciar algunas palabras como lo hacen los loros y las **guacamayas**. Así que en la granja del señor Domson las cosas eran verdaderamente muy raras. Si cualquier otra persona normal visitara esa granja pensaría que el señor Domson debía ser internado en un **manicomio** o en un centro **psiquiátrico**. Pero la verdad es que lleva una vida sana y tranquila, mucho más saludable que la de la mayoría de las personas que viven en grandes ciudades y tienen trabajos esclavizantes que no les gustan y los hacen **infelices**.

Una tarde mientras Domson trabajaba en el **huerto**, llegaron unos tipos en una **camioneta** blanca. Llamaron a gritos preguntando si había alguien y Domson salió a recibirlos. Había pasado mucho tiempo desde la última vez que habló con otros seres humanos. Estas personas eran miembros de una fundación de protección animal y medio ambiente, pero tenían un caso muy raro. Algo a lo que nunca se habían enfrentado, parecía un **fenómeno** paranormal y estaba relacionado con murciélagos.

Esta fundación se enteró de que Domson era toda una autoridad en materia de murciélagos y venían a solicitar su ayuda en este inusual y desconcertante caso. Los miembros de la fundación Natura Terra eran tres: el biólogo marino Carlos Acevedo, la veterinaria Eliza Lambada y el antropólogo Sergio Novelli. Tuvieron una conversación con el señor Domson.

Carlos Acevedo: Señor Domson, nosotros representamos a la fundación Natura Terra, encargada de proteger a los animales y el medio ambiente. No somos un grupo de ecologistas de una organización hippie. Somos científicos profesionales al servicio de la naturaleza.

Eliza Lambada: Hemos seguido estudiado y analizado sus trabajos con los murciélagos. Investigamos cada teoría que usted ha desarrollado sobre el comportamiento y la vida de estas especies. También sabemos que usted posee alguna clase de poderes, por decirlo así, que tienen que ver con las facultades y habilidades que tienen los murciélagos. Sergio Novelli: Hace una semana, se encontraron varios murciélagos de distintas especies muertos a la orilla de la playa y otros en ríos. A todos les faltaba el **ala** izquierda y tenían una marca de pintura en la cara.

Señor Domson: Bueno señores, creo que ahora me toca hablar a mí. Les **ruego** no me interrumpan con preguntas porque nunca jamás suelo hablar con otras personas. Así que antes de que me sigan explicando todo este **aberrante** y **vergonzoso** caso de exterminio de estas hermosas y fantásticas criaturas, déjenme **aclararles** algo primero. Solo haré el trabajo por los murciélagos, no por dinero. No pienso recibir ningún tipo de pago. No habrá **periodistas**. Nada de radio **prensa** o televisión. Una vez que me den toda la información, trabajaré solo. Ustedes se desaparecen hasta que yo resuelva todo esto.

Los miembros de Natura Terra escucharon y aceptaron todas las condiciones del Señor Domson. Le terminaron de contar todos los últimos **sucesos**, se **despidieron** le agradecieron y se fueron. Domson se quedó pensativo un largo rato. Fue a su biblioteca y revisó algunos de sus libros. Repasó varias de sus investigaciones pasadas y se comunicó con todos los murciélagos que habitaban en su **granja**. Ellos también participarán en esta investigación. Quien mejor que un murciélago para resolver crímenes sobre otros murciélagos?

Domson realizó varias expediciones a los ríos y a las playas donde habían aparecido los murciélagos muertos. Tomó muestras del agua y de las **piedras** de la arena - de todo. Vió a uno de esos muertos y les faltaba el ala izquierda tal y como dijeron los científicos y la cara manchada con pintura. Se llevó ese murciélago, mientras los **cuatrocientos ochenta** murciélagos que vivían con él volaban por todas las otras zonas inaccesibles para los humanos comunicándose con sus

parientes y mandando señales de ultrasonido a Domson sobre lo que iban descubriendo.

Lo que **hallaron** fue realmente sorprendente. En una de las cuevas vivía una criatura alucinante, mitad murciélago y mitad humano. La cara, los brazos y las manos eran de murciélago y tenía alas, pero el cuerpo, las piernas y los pies eran humanos. Emitía un extraño sonido pero también podía pronunciar palabras, frases y oraciones completas. Era fascinante pero no tenía nada que ver con las muertes de los otros murciélagos.

Cazadores humanos eran los que mataban a esos murciélagos y esta criatura llegaba siempre al lugar del crimen y **ahuyentaba** a los cazadores que salían espantados. Pero ya estaban muertos, él les **arrancaba** el ala izquierda para realizar un ritual de protección para estas especies tan amenazadas. Domson decidió no decirle nada a los científicos de Natura Terra y mantener en secreto la existencia de esta criatura hermosa y mágica.

English

Every night at 11 o'clock, Domson, who was eight years old, went out to the patio of his house and into the garden. He stood quietly, watching the tree because he knew that a bat was always hanging there. He liked to see him fly and get lost, confusing the bat with the darkness of the night. All bats look alike and also fly together in large flocks, but Domson was sure he always saw the same bat. He had the same capacity as these mammals, a high-frequency ultrasound system. Domson was a special child endowed with great faculties, and one of them was that he could locate any sound. Every night at 11 o'clock, Domson put some pieces of chopped fruit on the bat. Time passed, and the little boy of eight years grew up. Now, Domson was a 40-year-old man and never stopped interacting with bats. He developed a strong bond with bats, a special connection. He understood the bats, and the bats understood him. It was a perfect communication, much better and more sincere than that of humans. Throughout his life, Domson was the victim of mockery and humiliation for loving bats so much. They believed that he was involved in some satanic cult, but Domson never paid attention to those attacks because he knew they were the product of ignorance and mediocrity.

Domson worked in an advertising and marketing agency but left everything to devote himself to the study of these mammals. He grabbed all his savings and bought a farm to raise, care for, and receive bats that came from everywhere. He was a lonely man: he had not married or had a partner or friends. His only company was the bats. So intimate and strong was the relationship he had with them that he developed the same customs over time—he slept the same way and ate only fruits and rye bread

He was not blind. He had a good vision, and his eyes were very healthy. However, he spent days with his eyes covered with a thick, black cloth to develop and sharpen his other senses. Each time, he looked more like a bat and less like a human. But the really strange thing was that sometimes, the bats looked human. They learned to pronounce some words as parrots and macaws do. So on Mr. Domson's farm, things were really very strange. If any other normal person visited that farm, they would think that Mr. Domson should be admitted to a mental hospital or a psychiatric center. But the truth is that he led a healthy and quiet life, much healthier than most people who live in big cities and have enslaving jobs that they don't like and make them unhappy. One afternoon, while Domson worked in the vegetable garden, some guys arrived in a white van. They called loudly, asking if there was anyone, and Domson came out to meet them. It had been a long time since he last spoke with other human beings. These people were members of an animal and environmental protection foundation, but they had a very rare case, something they had never faced. It seemed a paranormal phenomenon and was related to bats.

This foundation learned that Domson was an authority on bats and came to ask for his help in this unusual and disconcerting case. The members of the Natura Terra Foundation were three: marine biologist Carlos Acevedo, veterinarian Eliza Lambada, and anthropologist Sergio Novelli. They had a conversation with Mr. Domson.

Carlos Acevedo: "Mr. Domson, we represent the Natura Terra Foundation, in charge of protecting animals and the environment. We are not a group of environmentalists of a hippie organization. We are professional scientists at the service of nature." Eliza Lambada: "We have continued to study and analyze your work with bats. We investigated every theory that you have developed about the behavior and life of these species. We also know that you have some kind of powers, so to speak, that have to do with the faculties and abilities that bats have." Sergio Novelli: "A week ago, several bats of different species were found dead on the shore of the beach and others in rivers. They all lacked the left wing and had a face paint mark.

Mr. Domson: "Well, gentlemen, I think it's my turn to talk to me now. I beg you; don't interrupt me with questions because

I never talk to other people. So before you continue to explain to me all about this aberrant and shameful case of extermination of these beautiful and fantastic creatures, let me clarify something first. I will only do the work for the bats, not for money. I will not receive any payment. There will be no journalists, no radio, press, or television. Once you give me all the information, I will work alone. You disappear until I solve all this."

The members of Natura Terra listened and accepted all the conditions of Mr. Domson. They finished telling him all the latest events, said goodbye, thanked him, and left. Domson thought for a long time. He went to his library and reviewed some of his books. He reviewed several of his past investigations and communicated with all the bats that inhabited his farm. They would also participate in this research. Who better solve crimes about other bats than a bat?

Domson made several expeditions to the rivers and beaches where the dead bats had appeared. He sampled water and beach stones—everything. He saw one of those dead bats, and they lacked the left wing, as the scientists said. Also, their faces were stained with paint. He took that bat, while the four hundred and eighty bats that lived with him flew through the other areas inaccessible to humans, communicating with their relatives and sending ultrasound signals to Domson about what they were discovering.

What they found was really amazing. In one of the caves lived an amazing creature, half-bat and half-human. The face, arms, and hands were of a bat and had wings, but the body, legs, and feet were human. It made a strange sound but could also pronounce words, phrases, and complete sentences. It

40

was fascinating, but it had nothing to do with the deaths of the other bats.

Human hunters were the ones who killed those bats, and this creature always arrived at the scene of the crime and scared away the hunters. But they were already dead. He tore their left wings off to perform a ritual of protection for the threatened species. Domson decided not to tell Natura Terra scientists anything and kept the existence of this beautiful and magical creature secret.

Preguntas (Questions)

¿A qué edad empezó Domson a relacionarse con los murciélagos?

1. a los 22 años

2. a los 15 años

3. a los 8 años

¿En donde trabajaba Domson antes de dedicar su vida a los murciélagos?

1. una agencia de publicidad y mercadeo

2. en una heladería

3. en una fábrica de autos

¿Como se llama la veterinaria del grupo?

1. Anabela Lister

2. Rebeca Alonso

3. Eliza Lambada

At what age did Domson begin to interact with bats?

1. At age 22 years old

2. At age 15 years old

3. At age 8 years old

4. Where Domson worked before devoting his life to bats?

5. an advertising and marketing agency

6. in an ice cream shop

7. in a car factory

8. What is the group veterinarian's name?

9. Anabela Lister

10. Rebeca Alonzo

11. Eliza Lambada

¿TE CONOZCO? - DO I KNOW YOU?

Vocabulary

Spanish	Pronunciation	English
Sienta	See-AN-tah	Sits
Sabes	SAH-bays	You know
Cosas	COH-sahs	Things
Por Cierto	POUR-see AIR-toe	By the way
Todavía	Toe-dah-VEE-ah	Still
Explicar	ExPLEE-car	Explain
Imaginaria	Ee-mag-ee-NAIR-riah	Imaginary
Pequeño	Pay-KAIN-noh	Small
Nunca	NOON-kah	Never

Daniel va en el bus hacia su casa cuando una chica se **sienta** a su lado. Él no le presta atención a la niña y continúa saliendo por la ventana. Se concentró en una cosa, y eso era llegar a casa. Tenía grandes planes para el fin de semana. "Hola Daniel." "Eh... ¿Cómo **sabes** me nombre?" Daniel preguntó. "Soy Gaby. Y sé muchas **cosas**. Como que tu color favorito es el azul." "¿Cómo **sabes** eso?" "Y que te gustan las películas de acción." "Sí, pero..."

*Daniel is on the bus to his house when a girl **sits** down next to him. He doesn't pay the girl any attention and continues*

44

*to stare out the window. He focused on one thing, and that was getting home. He had big plans for the weekend. "Hello, Daniel." "Eh... How do **you know** my name?" Daniel asked. "I am Gaby, and I know many **things**. Like that your favorite color is blue." "How do **you know** that?" "And that you like action movies." "Yes, but..."*

"¿Cómo está Toby, **por cierto**?" "¡¿Quién te dijo el nombre de mi perro?!" "¿Las hamburguesas son tu comida favorita **todavía**?" "¿Cómo **sabes** tanto de mí? ¿Y por qué no me respondes?" La joven le sonrió a Daniel, pero no respondió. Se sentó en silencio al lado de Daniel mientras el autobús se detenía tras otra. Daniel estaba cansada de esperar a que ella hablara y rompió el silencio, "Quiero saber cómo sabes tanto de mí." "Es un poco difícil de **explicar**. Bueno, aquí te bajas. Tu mama te está esperando. ¡Hasta luego!"

*"How is Toby, **by the way**?" "How do you know the name of my dog" "Are hamburgers your favorite food, **still**?" "How do **you know** so much about me? And why don't you answer me?" The young girl smiled at Daniel, but didn't respond. She sat quietly next to Daniel as the bus made stop after to stop. Daniel was tired of waiting for her to speak and broke the silence. "I want to know how you know so much about me." "It is a little difficult to **explain**. Well, here is your stop. Your mother is waiting for you. See you later."*

Daniel se baja del bus y le explica a su mama lo que pasó. "Gaby era el nombre de tu amiga **imaginaria** cuando eras **pequeño**. Obviamente, ella **nunca** existió," mamá de Daniel explicada. "Pues esta niña sí existe. Estaba sentada a mi lado." "Daniel... yo vi por la ventana del bus. Y nadie estaba contigo." La mama de Daniel le peinó amorosamente hacia atrás. Había sido una semana larga en la escuela, así que debía de estar cansado. "Tal vez soñaste con ella," le ofreció su madre. "No me dormí... al menos no creo que la haya hecho." "No nos preocupemos por eso cariño. ¿Por qué no vamos a comer algo y hablamos de lo que quieres hacer este fin de semana?" Daniel asintió de acuerdo. Debió de estar cansado en el autobús y su mente había sacado lo mejor de él, pero aún le hizo temblar pensar que alguien sabía mucho de él.

*Daniel gets off the bus and tells his mother what happened. "Gaby was the name of your **imaginary** friend when you were **little**. Obviously, she **never** existed," Daniel's mother explained. "Well, this girl does exist. She was sitting next to me." "Daniel... I saw through the window of the bus, and no one was next to you." Daniel's mom lovingly brushed his hair back. It had been a long week at school, so he must have been tired. "Maybe you dreamt about her," his mom offered. "I didn't fall asleep... At least I don't think I did." "Let's not worry about it honey. Why don't we go get a snack and talk about what you want to do this weekend?" Daniel nodded in agreement. He must have been tired on the bus and his mind had gotten the best of him, but it still made him shiver to think somebody knew that much about him.*

Resumen de la historia

Una chica llamada Gaby comienza a hablar con Daniel en el autobús y conoce mucha información personal sobre él. Esto lo sorprende, pero ella no le dirá cómo sabe esa información. Cuando se baja del bus, le dice a su madre lo que sucedió, pero ella dice que Gaby era su amiga imaginaria y que no había nadie sentado a su lado.

Summary of the story

A girl named Gaby starts talking to Daniel on the bus and knows a lot of personal information about him. This shocks him, but she won't tell him how she knows that information. When he gets off the bus, he tells his mother what happened, but she says that Gaby was his imaginary friend and that there wasn't anybody sitting next to him.

Respuestas (Answers)

    a. A

    b. C

    c. B

    d. D

EL PUEBLO DE CALAVERA

El Lejano Oeste era famoso por su historia sangrienta. Deadwood, Dakota del Sur; San Antonio, Texas; Tombstone, Arizona... había muchos pueblos peligrosos y sin ley. En algunos casos, el sheriff del pueblo era la persona más poderosa. Mantenía el orden público.

Pero no todos los pueblos tenían un sheriff.

Por ejemplo, ¡Calavera, Oklahoma! Calavera no tenía sheriff, ni leyes, ni reglas. No era civilizado en absoluto. Cada uno hacía lo que quería.

Había apuestas, peleas, bebida, y otros vicios durante el día y la noche, siete días a la semana. La mayoría de los días, había un asesinato antes del desayuno. ¡O durante el desayuno!

Aun así, el pueblo seguía creciendo cada año. Y cada año, había un criminal nuevo que llegaba y trataba de tomar el control. Trataban de convertirse en los jefes de Calavera, los jefes de todos los habitantes del lugar.

Para controlar el crimen, debías ser más duro que los otros criminales. Para hacer dinero, debías desearlo más que los demás.

Por eso los jefes nunca vivían demasiado tiempo. ¡Siempre los mataban y los reemplazaban!

Hasta que un día, a finales del otoño, llegó Erkek Tex.

49

Las personas que vivían allí, los habitantes de Calavera, supieron inmediatamente que traería problemas. Se dieron cuenta cuando lo vieron entrar al pueblo montado a caballo. El caballo era pálido, más blanco que la leche. El hombre tenía la cara curtida como el cuero, la piel bronceada por el sol. Bajo la nariz tenía un bigote negro gigante. El bigote le llegaba hasta debajo de los labios. Las cejas eran tan tupidas como el bigote.

—¿De dónde piensas que vino ese hombre? —le preguntó el dueño de la tienda a su amigo. El amigo era el dueño del bar que estaba al otro lado de la calle. El bar se llamaba Salón Brisas de la Pradera.

—No es de por aquí —dijo el dueño del bar—. Parece extranjero.

—Pues bien, Marty, ¿de qué país crees que viene?

Marty alzó las manos. No lo sabía.

El dueño de la tienda miró a Erkek Tex. Tex estaba atando su caballo blanco a un poste. El sol se ponía y el viento ya era frío. Tex sacó una caja pequeña. Cogió un poco de tabaco y armó un cigarro. Inclinó la cabeza para encender el cigarro. Un sombrero de vaquero grande y marrón le cubría los ojos.

Cuando volvió a mirar hacia arriba, Tex estaba mirando a Marty, el dueño del bar.

—Si tú estás sentado aquí, ¿quién cuida tu bar? —preguntó. Tenía un acento muy fuerte, sonaba como una persona del Oriente Medio. Jamás se lo diría a nadie en el pueblo, pero su familia había emigrado desde el Imperio Otomano. De hecho, su sobrenombre, «Erkek», significaba «hombre» en turco.

50

—Trato de quedarme afuera —dijo Marty—. En mi bar, los clientes cogen lo que quieren, y pagan lo que quieren. Si no, hay problemas.

—¿Qué quieres decir con «problemas»?

—Quiero decir que ya les han disparado a los últimos tres dueños del Salón Brisas de la Pradera.

—Vuelve al bar —dijo Erkek Tex—. Voy a entrar. Y no me gusta servirme mis propias bebidas.

El dueño del bar miró a Tex. Tex no era corpulento, pero tampoco era pequeño. Tenía músculos, pero su cuerpo era delgado. Llevaba pistolas a ambos lados del cuerpo.

—Forastero —dijo Marty—, iré al bar, pero no empieces a dispararle a las personas. No quiero tener problemas.

—Yo tampoco quiero problemas —dijo Tex—. Por eso no habrá ninguno.

El dueño del bar era también el camarero (la persona que servía las bebidas). Cruzó la calle caminando. Dentro del Salón Brisas de la Pradera había una docena de hombres. Algunos estaban jugando un juego de cartas. Otros estaban sentados a las mesas, sosteniendo vasos o botellas. Algunos otros estaban sentados junto a la barra larga de madera del bar, hablando en voz alta. Cuando vieron entrar al dueño del bar, se detuvieron.

—¡Sal de aquí, Marty! —dijo uno de los hombres sentados junto a la barra. Era alto y tenía el cabello marrón, largo y rizado. También tenía barba marrón. Vestía ropas desgastadas y olía muy mal. Dejó su taburete y se puso de pie—. Ponemos nuestro dinero sobre la barra. Cogemos lo que queremos beber, así que no te necesitamos.

—Está bien —dijo el dueño del bar—, solamente vine a ver cómo estaban las cosas.

El hombre con rizos a quien llamaban «Curly» caminó hacia Marty. Le puso una mano sobre el pecho.

—Te dije que no te necesitamos. No hay nada para que vengas a ver. Ahora te puedes ir.

El amigo de Curly se rio.

—Sí, ¡déjanos solos, viejo!

Marty frunció el ceño y se dio la vuelta para volver a salir. Pero en ese momento, entró Erkek Tex.

Tex miró al hombre con el cabello rizado.

—Camarero —dijo Tex con voz muy gruesa—, hoy he viajado muchas millas a caballo. Tengo mucha sed. No te quedes ahí parado y sírveme una bebida.

Curly escupió en el suelo.

—¡No soy el camarero!

—Entonces, ¿dónde está el camarero? ¡Estoy cansado de esperar!

Curly señaló a Marty.

—Este es el camarero, pero no lo queremos aquí adentro.

—Está bien —dijo Tex—. Si él se va, entonces tú puedes servirme mi bebida. ¡Ya!

Curly sacó su pistola y le apuntó a Erkek Tex.

—Nadie me habla de esa ma...

El sonido de un disparo se hizo eco en el bar. Curly cayó muerto al suelo.

—¿Quién será el camarero? —preguntó Tex, con la pistola humeante en la mano.

Todos apuntaron a Marty.

English

The Far West was famous for its bloody history. Deadwood, South Dakota; San Antonio, Texas; Tombstone, Arizona ... there were many dangerous and lawless towns. In some cases, the town sheriff was the most powerful person. Maintained public order.

But not all towns had a sheriff.

For example, Skull, Oklahoma! Calavera had no sheriff, no laws, no rules. He was not civilized at all. Each one did what he wanted.

There were bets, fights, drinks, and other vices during the day and night, seven days a week. Most days, there was a murder before breakfast. Or during breakfast!

Even so, the town kept growing every year. And every year, there was a new criminal who came and tried to take control. They tried to become the chiefs of Calavera, the chiefs of all the inhabitants of the place.

To control the crime, you had to be harder than the other criminals. To make money, you should want it more than others.

That's why bosses never lived too long. They always killed them and replaced them!

Until one day, at the end of autumn, Erkek Tex arrived.

The people who lived there, the inhabitants of Calavera, knew immediately that it would bring problems. They realized when they saw him enter the horse-riding town. The horse was pale, whiter than milk. The man had a tanned face like leather, skin tanned by the sun. Under his nose he had a giant black mustache. The mustache reached to his lips. The eyebrows were as thick as the mustache.

"Where do you think that man came from?" The store owner asked his friend. The friend was the owner of the bar that was across the street. The bar was called Salón Brisas de la Pradera.

"It's not from here," said the owner of the bar. It seems foreign.

"Well, Marty, what country do you think is coming from?"

Marty raised his hands. I did not know, I did not know it.

The store owner looked at Erkek Tex. Tex was tying his white horse to a pole. The sun was setting and the wind was already cold. Tex took out a small box. He took some tobacco and put together a cigar. He bowed his head to light the cigar. A big brown cowboy hat covered his eyes.

Tex looked at the man with curly hair.

"Waiter," Tex said very thickly, "today I traveled many miles on horseback. I'm so thirsty. Do not stand there and pour me a drink.

Curly spat on the floor.

"I am not the waiter!"

"So where is the waiter?" I'm tired of waiting!

Curly pointed at Marty.

"This is the waiter, but we don't want him in here."

"It's all right," Tex said. If he leaves, then you can pour me my drink. Already!

Curly pulled out his gun and aimed it at Erkek Tex.

"Nobody tells me about that ma ...

The sound of a shot echoed in the bar. Curly fell dead to the ground.

"Who will be the waiter?" Asked Tex, the smoking gun in his hand.

Everyone pointed to Marty.

Resumen

El pueblo de Calavera, Oklahoma es muy peligroso porque no hay sheriff. No hay nadie a cargo del pueblo. Un vaquero misterioso llamado Erkek Tex llega al pueblo. Le pide a Marty, el dueño del bar del pueblo, que entre al bar. Tex entra. Ve que los clientes no quieren que Marty esté allí. Uno de los clientes le apunta a Tex, pero Tex lo mata primero.

Vocabulario

- sangriento/a - cruel, bloody
- la apuesta - bet
- el vicio - bad habit
- creciendo - growing
- los reemplazaban - they replaced them
- curtido/a - tanned
- tupido/a - thick
- el vaquero - cowboy
- el sobrenombre - nickname
- el forastero - stranger
- sosteniendo - holding
- desgastado/a - worn out
- no te quedes parado - don't stand still
- humeante - smoky

Preguntas De Selección Múltiple

Selecciona una respuesta para cada pregunta

1. La familia de Erkek Tex viene de:

    a. Oklahoma

    b. México

    c. Deadwood, Dakota del Sur

    d. el Imperio Otomano

2. En el pueblo, Marty es dueño de:

a. la tienda

b. el establo para caballos

c. el bar

d. la peluquería

3. ¿De qué color es el caballo de Tex?

a. Blanco

b. Marrón

c. Negro

d. Gris oscuro

4. ¿Por qué Marty se sienta afuera?

a. Confía en sus clientes

b. Tiene miedo de sus clientes

c. No tiene ningún cliente

d. Hay una persona que sirve a los clientes

5. ¿Qué quiere Curly?

a. Servirle una bebida a Tex

b. Que Marty se vaya

c. Que Marty le sirva una bebida a Tex

d. Matar a Marty y a Tex

Respuestas Al Capítulo 1

1. d

2. c

3. a

4. b

5. b

CPSIA information can be obtained
at www.ICGtesting.com
Printed in the USA
BVHW091504190521
607631BV00001B/7